So You Want To Impress!!!!

By Steven M. Topple

© 2005 Steven M. Topple. All Rights Reserved.

No part of this book may be reproduced, stored in a retrieval system, or transmitted by any means without the written permission of the author.

First published by AuthorHouse 10/12/05

ISBN: 1-4208-8381-X (sc)

Printed in the United States of America
Bloomington, Indiana

This book is printed on acid-free paper.

authorHOUSE

1663 Liberty Drive
Bloomington, Indiana 47403
(800) 839-8640
www.authorhouse.com

SO YOU WANT TO IMPRESS!!!!

So You Want to Impress!!!!
By Steven M Topple

A simple guide to impressive dining.

Hello and thank you for choosing **So You Want to Impress!!!!**

There are so many cookbooks to pick up and select from, but you decided to choose this one. I hope you enjoy reading it and preparing the recipes.

My passion for writing this book: I love to cook; no really, I love to cook! I love to make people happy with food. When I see people with a big smile after taking a bite of food, it makes it all worthwhile

People come into my restaurant and often say, "Do you have a cookbook or do you have the recipes for this great food that we have eaten."

So I said to myself, I want to create and write my **own** *cookbook. I have always wanted to write a cookbook.*

I have quite a few friends out there who have been 100 percent behind me in completing this project.

I always love going to or cooking for private dinner parties. So this cookbook has been written with this in mind. So you want to impress people at private dinner parties, this is where the name of the cookbook came from.

I am originally from Portsmouth, England. Portsmouth is a famous naval port and it has lots of great history. It is not really known for its food or fine creations of food.

I went to an excellent culinary school in Portsmouth, called Highbury College.
The passion for my career was formed there, super teachers of food, too many teachers to name, but the one who meant the most to me was Mr. Paul Self.

I then went to work in London with the famous chefs, which they talk about at culinary school. I worked in Scotland for a while, then my dream came true and I found myself working in the USA.

I have been in the United States for six years. I have worked in several different parts of the United States: Georgia, Upstate New York, San Francisco, South Carolina, and last but not least Vail, Colorado.
You will find out a little bit more about my history and where I worked throughout this book.

The book

I have broken the book into seven different meal periods and times of the year.
Some of the recipes are in a menu form for you to follow and create a super meal; you could, of course, create your own menu from the recipes.

Below are the chapters that you will find in the book:

Breakfast recipes
Lunch recipes

Vegetarian Menu (This is a section that is very dear to me. My parents are both vegetarian, so I always try new dishes out on them. These are ones they like a lot. They turned vegetarian about twelve years ago; they understand the reason for me not turning vegetarian as well.)

Spring Menu
Summer Menu
Fall Menu
Winter Menu

All of my recipes are very easy to moderate and make.
The products are available at most grocery stores, good butchers, and fish stores.

Have a go at making these, and if you like them, make the meals for your friends and impress them!

If you have any questions about the recipes or menus, please contact me at the Web address given inside this book.

Happy cooking and enjoy.

Steve Topple

Sebastian and myself enjoying the final picture taking

Acknowledgments

*First, my wonderful **parents** who have done so much for me in my life, and for being there to support me and having faith in me with so many different things I do. I just want you to know how much I appreciate all that you do. I love you!!!*

*Second, my photographer, **Mr. Sebastian Maturana**, thank you so much for all your help. I would never have gotten this done without your help; the photos look great.*

*Third, my dear American **Paulette**, thank you for your belief in me; all your prayers have worked, thank you.*

*Fourth a big Thank you to my **grandparents** and **brother** for being there for me. I love you all so much.*

*Fifth the **Lodge at Vail** and all there staff for letting me use the hotel for some pictures.*

Last but not least, my line cooks, thank you all for your support. You may not think that I appreciate you, but trust me I do, and you make me look good lots of times. All I can say is keep the faith and keep pushing all the time; you will see the rewards

Chef Steve Inspecting the plate's before being eating.

Contents of So You Want to Impress!!!

So you have some guests for the morning. 1

Strawberry Stuffed French Toast   2
Smoked Salmon Scrambled Egg   4
Vermont Cheddar and Ham Burrito with Tomato Salsa   6
Banana and Chocolate Chip Pancakes   8
Poached Egg with Potato Hash and Hollandaise Sauce   10
Mountain Blueberry Granola 12

Some guests are coming for lunch   15

Chilled Honeydew and Ginger Soup with a Pineapple Salsa   16
Pan-Roasted Free Range Chicken Spinach Salad And a Sherry Bacon Vinaigrette 18
Lime-marinated Jumbo Lump Crab Quesadilla   20
Roasted Tomato and Basil Soup   22
Marinated Strawberries with Vanilla Mascarpone Cream   24
Roasted Potato, Green Onion Salad with Grain Mustard Vinaigrette   26
Chocolate Chip Cookies   28

So vegetarian what are you going to make them? 31

Potato and Celery Root Lasagna with Chive Butter Sauce   32
Salsify and Squash Linguine with Parmesan Sauce 34
Spinach and Mushroom Tortellini with Tomato and Pesto Sauce   36
Spinach Gnocchi with Tomato and Tarragon Sauce 38

The seasonal menus: I have chosen these menus for you, but you can pick and choose yourself. All are well balanced and very easy to make.

Spring Menu 41

Jumbo Lump Crab Cake with Vanilla Mango Chutney And Lemon Thyme Vinaigrette   42
Wild Oregon Salmon with Tarragon and Orange Risotto   44
Vanilla Crème Brulee 46
Asparagus Strudel, Frisee Salad, and Red Pepper Coulis   48
Spring Lamb Chops with Celery Root Potato and Mint Sauce   50
Warm Peach Tart Tatin with Vanilla Ice Cream   52

Summer Menu   55

Dungeness Crab and Apple Tower with Lemon Thyme Vinaigrette 56
Pan-roasted Free Range Chicken, Spinach Potato And Tarragon Sauce   58
Rhubarb Crumble with Vanilla Ice Cream   60
Goat Cheese and Chive Spring Roll with Pesto Dressing   62
Poached Halibut with Red Pepper Couscous and Spinach Sauce   64
Strawberry Crepe with Crème Chantilly   66

Fall Menu   69

Forest Mushroom Soup with Truffle Cream   70
Roast Veal Chop with Truffle Risotto 72
Orange Crème Brulee 74
Potato Crusted Foie Gras, Pear Chutney and a Cherry Sauce   76
Pecan-crusted Venison Loin, Apple Potato Puree and a Blackberry Sauce 78
Banana Bread Pudding with Vanilla Custard 80

Winter Menu 83

Curried Butternut Squash Soup with Chive Crème Friache 84
Roast Beef Wellington with Horseradish Potato And Red Wine Sauce   86
Flourless Chocolate Fondant Cake   88
Pan Seared Diver Scallops with Saffron Risotto   90
Marinated Duck Breast with Napa Cabbage and Raspberry Sauce 92
Port Poached Pear with Cinnamon Whipped Cream 94

Metric Conversion Chart

This chart is your use if you want to change anything to different measurements

Oven Temperatures

American Standard	Metric
250° F	130° C
300° F	150° C
350° F	180° C
400° F	200° C
450° F	230° C

Volume (Dry)

American Standard	Metric
1/8 teaspoon	.5 ml
1/4 teaspoon	1 ml
1/2 teaspoon	2 ml
3/4 teaspoon	4 ml
1 teaspoon	5 ml
1 tablespoon	15 ml
1/4 cup	59 ml
1/3 cup	79 ml
1/2 cup	118 ml
2/3 cup	158 ml
3/4 cup	177 ml
1 cup	225 ml
2 cups or 1 pint	450 ml
3 cups	675 ml
4 cups or 1 quart	1 liter
1/2 gallon	2 liters
1 gallon	4 liters

Volume (Liquid)

American Standard (Cups & Quarts)	American Standard (Ounces)	Metric (Milliliters & Liters)
2 tbsp	1 fl. oz.	30 ml
1/4 cup	2 fl. oz.	60 ml
1/2 cup	4 fl. oz.	125 ml
1 cup	8 fl. oz.	250 ml
1 1/2 cups	12 fl. oz.	375 ml
2 cups or 1 pint	16 fl. oz.	500 ml
4 cups or 1 quart	32 fl. oz.	1000 ml or 1 liter
1 gallon	128 fl. oz.	4 liters

Weight (Mass)

American Standard (Ounces)	Metric (Grams)
1/2 ounce	15 grams
1 ounce	30 grams
3 ounces	85 grams
3.75 ounces	100 grams
4 ounces	115 grams
8 ounces	225 grams
12 ounces	340 grams
16 ounces or 1 lb.	450 grams

Chef Steve organizing the ticket's for a busy night at the restaurant

Chapter 1

So you have some guests for the morning.

And you want to impress!!!!

Strawberry Stuffed French Toast

What A great breakfast dish, Give your guests something to remember, there stay at your house.

Makes 4

Ingredients

8 slices white bread, crust taken off
6 eggs, cracked and beaten, with 1 oz. of milk
½ cup of caster (superfine) sugar
2 cups of water
2 pints of fresh strawberries
1 teaspoon of vanilla extract
1 oz. of soft butter

To Garnish

2 cups of heavy whipping cream (whipped lightly)
1 tablespoon of powdered sugar
4 sprigs of mint

Method

In a small saucepan, place the water, vanilla, and caster sugar. Bring to a boil and turn down to a simmer. Preheat a nonstick pan.

Place the sliced white bread on a sheet tray. Slice the strawberries long ways, removing the stems, and place in the middle of the bread. Place another piece of bread on top.
Meanwhile, place the butter into the nonstick pan.

Dip the stuffed French toast into the egg mixture, then place into the pan with the butter.
Cut the remaining strawberries into quarters, and then add to the syrup reduction from earlier. Stop cooking when a pink color has been achieved and the mixture sticks to the back of the spoon.

Turn the French toast over after 2 minutes, and after a further 2 minutes, remove from the pan.
Slice the bread on the angle long diagonally cut.
Serve the toast on a warmed plate with the strawberry syrup and the vanilla whipped cream. Dust the plate with a little powdered sugar and mint sprig.
Enjoy.

Smoked Salmon Scrambled Egg

Every body loves smoked salmon and everybody loves scrambled egg, so why not combine these together, try it out. You could even put caviar on top if you want to take this over the top.

Makes 4

Ingredients

4 slices wheat bread
6 eggs, cracked and beaten with 1 oz. of milk
2 oz. of smoked salmon
1 oz. of soft butter
Salt and pepper to taste

To Garnish

½ cup of crème friache
4 sprigs of parsley

Method

Preheat a nonstick pan with the soft butter.

Place the beaten egg in the pan. Keep stirring until the egg begins to scramble.
Meanwhile toast the bread, butter and cut into diagonal pieces.

Slice the smoked salmon into very thin strips add to the egg in the pan. Season the egg and salmon with salt and pepper—remember, the salmon may be salty.
Remove the scrambled egg from the heat, then place onto the buttered toast.

Place onto a nice warmed plate, and place a little crème fraiche and the parsley sprigs on top of each plate. Serve and enjoy.

Vermont Cheddar and Ham Burrito with Tomato Salsa

A great breakfast dish if you had some friends over for the night. Give your guests something fast and fun, this has the taste of a warm sunny morning in sunny Mexico.
Very simple to complete.

Makes 4

Ingredients

4 tortilla wraps
4 eggs, cracked and beaten with 1 oz. of milk
2 oz. of diced and cooked ham
2 oz. of Vermont cheddar, grated
1 oz. of soft butter
Salt and pepper to taste

To Garnish

2 large tomatoes
1 small onion peeled and small diced
1 clove of garlic peeled
½ cup of blended oil
Salt and pepper to taste
Add all the ingredients to a food processor until a smooth chunky salsa is made

Method

Preheat a nonstick pan with the soft butter.

Place the beaten egg in the pan. Keep stirring until the egg begins to scramble.
Add the ham to the pan and season with salt and pepper.

Meanwhile, warm the tortillas wraps in an oven set at 350 f for 2 minutes, and then place the scrambled egg in the middle of the wrap. Sprinkle with the grated cheddar cheese.

Roll up into a wrap. Start with the sides, then roll, cut into halves on the diagonal.
Place onto a warmed plate, and place a little salsa over each burrito.

Serve and enjoy.

Banana and Chocolate Chip Pancakes

Something a little more filling. Every body loves pancakes, give these a try, show your guests what you can do early in the morning, the smell alone will wake them up.

Makes 4

Ingredients

½ cup of wheat flour
½ cup of quick-cooking oats
2 tsp. of baking powder
1 tsp. of sugar
¼ tsp. of ground cinnamon
1 tsp. of Blended oil
1 cup of milk
1 egg
2 medium sliced bananas
½ cup of chocolate chips
Syrup of your choice
Mint to garnish (optional)
Powdered sugar to garnish (optional)

Method

In a mixing bowl, mix the flour, oats, baking powder, sugar, and cinnamon. Stir all these together.

Add in the oil, egg, and milk until a smooth, not lumpy batter has been made.

Preheat a griddle or a large nonstick pan. Spray with a nonstick spray. Use a ladle to scoop the batter, to make 4-inch round pancakes. Sprinkle the banana slices onto the pancakes along with the chocolate chips.

Turn over when bubbles start to form on the top of the pancakes (2 minutes). The pancakes should be golden brown on top. Remove from the heat.

Serve the pancakes on a warmed plate with the syrup of your choice. Dust the plate with a little powdered sugar and mint sprig for garnish. Enjoy.

Poached Egg with Potato Hash and Hollandaise Sauce

A great breakfast dish; this is a take on eggs benedict, substituting a potato hash for the muffin. Every body always orders this when they go to a restaurant, why pay lots of money for when you can make this at home

Makes 4

Ingredients

8 whole
2 large Yukon gold potatoes, peeled
½ cup of white wine vinegar
1 small onion, peeled and diced
3 egg yolks
3 cups of melted clarified butter
4 cups of water
1 tablespoon of blended oil
Salt and pepper to taste

Method

Boil the potatoes in a small saucepan. When cooked remove the potatoes, grate using the large grate side of the grater.
In a small sauté pan, cook the onion in a little oil, until golden brown. Add the grated potato to the onion and continue cooking until golden brown. Remember to season.

In a small bowl, mix the egg yolks with 1 tablespoon of the white vinegar. Beat until very white and creamy. Add a little heat to the bowl over a flame or a pan of boiling water.
Slowly add the butter to the egg yolk mix. Keep whisking vigorously until thick and creamy. If the mix looks like it is going to break, (breaking means when the butter does not want to emulsify with the egg yolk mix) add a little water to thin down this help to prevent the mix breaking and it will help to hold.

Meanwhile, bring a small, deep pan to a boil, and add the remaining water and vinegar.
When the water has to come to a rolling boil, add the whole eggs cracked into it. The eggs should form a nice poached shape; turn down the heat so that it does not boil over.
Remove the eggs once they reach your desired liking. If you want them runny, they will take about 3 minutes; for well done, 5-6 minutes.

Place the potato hash into a middle of a warmed bowl. Then place the poached eggs on top of the hash.
Spoon the hollandaise sauce over the egg.
Serve and enjoy.

Mountain Blueberry Granola

A great breakfast dish to wake your taste buds up early in the morning, also this is so healthy for you. You can make a big batch of this and let this store in an air tight container for up to two months.

Ingredients

Dry
4 cups of Irish oatmeal
½ cup of rye flour
¼ cup brown sugar
1 tablespoon of cinnamon
1 cup of pecans
½ cup of coconut
1 pint of fresh blueberries

Wet
½ cup of blended oil
¾ cup of wild honey
¼ teaspoon of vanilla

Method

Mix all the dry ingredients together in a small bowl. Mix the wet ingredients together in a different bowl. Then slowly add the wet to the dry product. Place on a parchment paper-lined baking tray and bake for 35-45 minutes at 350° F.

When cooled down, store in a plastic container with a tight-fitting lid.

Serve with a vanilla yogurt or milk and fresh blueberries.

Miscellaneous information that you might want to know about!

So where in the book does Steve talk about the green things on top of most of the dishes? Here.

Most of them happen to be Micro Celery or Micro Greens.
A lot of chefs use these now a lot to decorate dishes with.
It is the trendy thing to do.
Your guests will be talking about them if you use them as well.
So give them a try, try a small package.

I buy these from accompany called chefs garden.
They have some great products there; lots of really good chefs use them.
Lots of different produce to lots Micro Greens.
www.chefsgarden.com

Or you can call them 1800 289 4644

Thank you to Chefs' Garden.

CHAPTER 2

SOME GUESTS ARE COMING FOR LUNCH

AND YOU WANT TO IMPRESS!!!!

Chilled Honeydew and Ginger Soup with a Pineapple Salsa

This is such a great lunch or dinner soup, serve this when it is hot and sunny outside and you will know what I mean about refreshing.

Ingredients

1 large honeydew melon, ripe (riper tastes better)
2 oz. of fresh ginger, peeled and chopped, small dice
1 pint of water
1 cup of sugar
½ of a sweet pineapple, peeled and diced very small
¼ cup of fresh chopped chives
1 small shallot chopped into a small dice
¼ cup of white wine vinegar

Method

Peel the honeydew melon and cut into small cubes.

In a bowl, mix the sugar and water together until the sugar has been dissolved.
Place the melon into a drink blender and add the ginger.

Turn on the blender and slowly add the sugar water mix until it makes the melon into smooth puree. Repeat this until all the melon has been pureed, and then strain using a coarse strainer to allow some of the pulp to remain in the soup. If the soup seems a little thick add the remaining water-sugar mix.

Place into a fridge and chill for at least 2 hours.

Mix the pineapple in a small bowl with the shallot and chopped chives and vinegar.

To serve, place into a chilled bowl, then add the pineapple salsa.

Pan-Roasted Free Range Chicken Spinach Salad
And a Sherry Bacon Vinaigrette

This is nice summer lunch entrée salad; this can be a show dish that is really simple.
Free range chicken is so much better to use, better flavor.
You can make this with out the bacon for non pork eaters.

Serves 4

Ingredients

4 6-oz. free range chicken breasts, (available at most supermarkets or good butchers on pre-order)
3 cups of baby spinach
1 tablespoon prepared coarse-grain mustard
½ cup of sherry vinegar
2 slices of bacon cut into small strips, called lardons professionally
¼ cup of brown sugar
Salt and pepper
2 cups of blended oil

Method

Pre-warm a grill or a nonstick pan with a little oil and then place the seasoned (salt and pepper) chicken breast on the grill or pan for 5 minutes, turning occasionally. Then place in preheated oven at 350f for 10 minutes.

Take the bacon and crisp in a small frying pan. Remove the excess fat; when the bacon is crisp, add the sherry vinegar, reduce, and add the brown sugar. When the vinegar has thickened, remove from heat. Whisk the blended oil with the vinegar and bacon. Season the vinaigrette with salt and pepper.

On a warmed plate, place the spinach salad in the middle, then place the chicken breast on top and spoon the dressing around the plate. Enjoy.

Lime-marinated Jumbo Lump Crab Quesadilla

This is a great dish for lunch. This is so different to eat and make, the jumbo lump crab and lime go so well together and then the fresh salsa taste wow!

Serves 4

Ingredients

1 lb can of jumbo lump crab (available at all supermarkets)
4 large tortilla wraps
1½ small onions, diced fine
2 cloves of peeled garlic, crushed
6 large tomatoes, chopped
2 limes, zest and juice
2 tablespoons of fresh cilantro
1 oz. of butter
1 oz. of pepper jack cheese
Salt and pepper
1 roasted pepper, cut into thin strips
1 small shallot

Method

Mix the jumbo lump crab with the lime zest and juice in a small bowl. Lay the tortilla wrap on the table.
Sprinkle the crab on one side of the wrap, and add half of the pepper and the cheese.
Take one tablespoon of the cilantro and sprinkle this over the crab. Fold the tortilla over in half to achieve a half-moon shape.

In a food processor, add the chopped tomato along with the shallot. Chop for about 10 seconds; add the one remaining tablespoon of cilantro. Continue for about 20 seconds more, then season with salt and pepper. Strain the salsa through a thick-holed strainer to remove the skins.

Preheat a nonstick pan, add the butter, and then place the quesadilla. Cook until golden brown on both sides, then place into the oven at 350f for 5 minutes.

To serve, cut the quesadilla into three equal shapes then pour a spoon of the salsa over the top. Serve and enjoy.

Roasted Tomato and Basil Soup

This is such a simple soup to make and a great flavor every body loves a good tomato soup

Makes 6 servings

Ingredients

4 onions, peeled and diced
1 bunch of celery, washed and diced
10 plum tomatoes diced, riper the better for better taste
2 large Yukon gold potatoes, peeled and diced
5 cloves of garlic, peeled
½ cup of blended oil
Salt and pepper
5 leaves of fresh basil
2 cups of crème fraiche
½ cup of fresh chopped chives

Method

In a large pot, cook the onion, celery, potatoes, and garlic in a small amount of oil.
Cook with no color, (you want no browning on the vegetables) we call this sweated in the professional kitchen, for 10 minutes until soft and tender. Add the tomatoes and cook for a further 15 minutes. Add the water and basil to the pot.

Cook for 45 minutes and puree with a stick blender. Check the seasoning.

In a small bowl, mix the crème fraiche with the fresh chopped chives. Pour into a squeeze bottle. Pour the soup into a bowl; Pour the chive crème fraiche around to garnish.

Marinated Strawberries with Vanilla Mascarpone Cream

This is a great summer lunch dessert or you could use this for a long summer evening. Great California strawberries or Florida has great strawberries all year round really.

Makes 4

Ingredients

2 pints of fresh strawberries
½ cup of balsamic vinegar, aged (a little thick)
1 pint of fresh mascarpone cream
1 tablespoon of vanilla extract
2 sprigs of mint
¼ cup of powdered sugar

Method

Wash the strawberries, cut them into quarters, then place them into a bowl. Add the ½ cup of balsamic vinegar. Mix together and let marinate for 20 minutes.

In another small bowl, add the mascarpone cream; slowly add the vanilla extract until the cream is spoonable.

Cut the mint into very thin strips. The best way to do this is to lay all the mint leaves on a table and roll them up like a cigar, then cut them into very thin strips and add them to the strawberries. (There is another term called chiffonade which means really thin strips of herb)

Chill a small bowl, and then place the strawberries in the middle of the bowl. Place 1 small scoop of the vanilla mascarpone cream in the middle of the strawberries, and dust with a little powdered sugar. Place a sprig of mint on top.

Serve and enjoy.

Roasted Potato, Green Onion Salad with Grain Mustard Vinaigrette

This is a great dish for a summer lunch, or you can use this for a side for a heavier lunch. You can leave the bacon out of the recipe if you are a vegetarian.

Serves 4

Ingredients

1 lb. of red potatoes, washed and cut into quarters
4 bunches of green onions
2 slices of bacon, sliced into thin strips
1 tablespoon of prepared stone ground grain mustard
1 tablespoon of white wine vinegar
3 tablespoons of blended oil
Salt and pepper to taste
1 oz. chopped fresh rosemary

Method

Boil the washed potatoes until they are a little undercooked but not too hard.
Preheat oven to 450 degrees.
Strain the potatoes and dry them a little. Place them into a roasting/baking tray with a little oil.
Season the potatoes with salt and pepper and the chopped rosemary.
Place into the oven for 35 minutes. About halfway through that time, shake the pan a little so that the potatoes cook evenly.

Meanwhile, cook the bacon and green onion in a large sauté pan.
Once the potatoes are golden brown and delicious, remove from tray and mix into the bacon and green onion, then season the potatoes with salt and pepper.

In a small mixing bowl, mix the vinegar and the mustard together. Add the oil slowly to emulsify.

Mix the vinaigrette over the potato and stir. Serve in a small bowl or a bigger one for a side dish. Enjoy.

Chocolate Chip Cookies

This is a great lunch snack or a snack at any time of the day.

Makes 6

Ingredients

12 oz. of caster (superfine) sugar
12 oz. of brown sugar
1 lb. of butter
¼ oz. of salt
¼ teaspoon of baking soda
2 eggs
1½ lb. of flour
2 lbs. of chocolate chips

Method

Using a stand mixer or a hand mixer, complete the following:
Mix the butter, caster sugar and brown sugar until a cream is made.
Add in all the rest of the ingredients.
Once dough has been made, stop mixing. I normally let the dough rest for about 1 hour.
Using an ice cream scoop, scoop the cookie dough into small balls.
Place onto a greased baking tray; flatten down the ball so it is flat.
Bake at 350° F for 25 minutes.
Remove from the heat; let the cookies cool for a while.
Serve and enjoy.

Chef Steve enjoying the service in the kitchen

CHAPTER 3

SO VEGETARIAN WHAT ARE YOU GOING TO MAKE THEM?

AND YOU WANT TO IMPRESS!!!!

Potato and Celery Root Lasagna with Chive Butter Sauce

This is a great vegetarian entrée, a little heartier for those looking for something more filling. There is no pasta involved in this dish. I have substituted potato for the pasta.

Makes 4 servings

Ingredients

4 large Idaho potatoes, washed
1 large celery root
½ teaspoon of ground nutmeg
6 cups of heavy cream
2 cloves of garlic, crushed
Salt and pepper to taste
2 cups of grated mozzarella cheese
2 tablespoons of grated parmesan cheese

Sauce
2 shallots, diced very small
2 cloves of garlic, crushed and peeled
Salt and pepper to taste
2 tablespoons of shaved parmesan cheese (to garnish)
1 cup of white wine
1oz of butter
½ cup of chopped chives
½ cup of heavy cream

Method

Preheat oven to 350° F.

Meanwhile, use a 2-quart saucepan to cook the garlic until translucent. Add the 6 cups of cream and the nutmeg and cook for about 20 minutes, then strain. Season the potatoes with salt and pepper.

Peel the potatoes, and cut using a mandolin, into very thin slices. Peel the celery root using a large knife. I find this easier than a regular peeler. Slice in half and repeat the same process as the potatoes.

Using a Pyrex dish lay the potato in the bottom of the dish. Ladle some of the cream on top and season with salt and pepper. Add the celery root next, repeating the cream and seasoning. Keep repeating this process until you have about 8 layers of potato and celery root each. Then sprinkle the mozzarella cheese on top.
Place foil on top of the dish and place into the oven for about 35 minutes. Remove the foil and place back in to the oven to get golden brown. Remove and keep for serving.

Sauce

In a small saucepan, cook the shallot and garlic with a little oil until translucent with no color. Add the white wine and reduce it by ¾. Add cream reduce by ½ again; slowly add all the butter. Keep whisking so that the butter will not split on you. (If you leave the butter unattended the butter will not emulsify, and it will cause the sauce not to look to good or taste good.

Season with salt and pepper, and then add the chopped chives.

To serve

Cut the lasagna into 2-inch squares. Place onto a warmed plate and drizzle a spoonful of sauce around. Garnish with shaved parmesan and chopped chives Serve and enjoy the lasagna with no pasta.

Salsify and Squash Linguine with Parmesan Sauce

This is a great vegetarian entrée. Instead of pasta, I have substituted the salsify. The salsify resembles the pasta shape when you use a large peeler.

Makes 4 servings

Ingredients

4 sticks of fresh salsify
2 large green zucchini
2 large yellow squash
1 small onion, diced very small
1 clove of garlic, crushed
1 cup of white wine
1 cup of heavy whipping cream
2 tablespoons of grated parmesan cheese
1 tablespoon of fresh chopped chives
Salt and pepper to taste

Method

Heat a pan of salted water to boiling, as if you were cooking pasta.

Peel the salsify using a large peeler to remove the brown outer skin; discard the outer skin. Continue to peel the salsify until you are left with just the thin strips that resemble linguine shapes.

If you are not going to make this dish right away, you may want to keep the salsify in some milk to stop the salsify from going brown.

Meanwhile, use a 2-quart saucepan, cook the onion and garlic until translucent. Deglaze the pan with the white wine, reduce the wine by ¾, add the cream, and reduce until thick consistency has been achieved. Add 1 tablespoon of the grated parmesan cheese. Season with salt and pepper, strain, and keep for the finish of the dish.

Take the squash and zucchini and peel just like you did to the salsify. Place into the boiling water along with the salsify. Cook for about 1 minute. Remove, toss with the parmesan sauce and freshly chopped chives, and season with salt and pepper.

Warm a large bowl. Place the squash and salsify into the bowl and garnish with a little shaved parmesan. Serve and enjoy.

Spinach and Mushroom Tortellini with Tomato and Pesto Sauce

This is a great light vegetarian entrée very easy to make. Very impressive

Makes 4 servings

Ingredients

1 small pack of wonton skins
1 lb. of fresh forest mushrooms, (crimini, shiitake and oyster mushrooms) washed and cut into quarters
1 lb. of fresh spinach 2 tablespoons of fresh grated parmesan cheese
1 onion, small, diced
2 cloves of garlic
1 egg, beaten for egg wash
2 tablespoons of blended oil
4 large tomatoes, chopped into small chunks
1 spoonful of pesto sauce (recipe below)
Salt and pepper to taste

Pesto dressing

2 cups of fresh basil
1 clove of fresh garlic, peeled
¼ cup of fresh grated parmesan cheese
1 cup of blended oil
¼ cup of toasted pine nuts
Salt and pepper to taste

Combine all ingredients and blend in a food processor to make a smooth paste.

Method

Cook the mushrooms in a small amount of oil. Add the spinach to the mix. After it is wilted and soft, season with salt and pepper. Reserve for later.
In a small sauté pan, cook the onion with the garlic until translucent; add the chunks of tomato to the onion pan.

Continue to cook for about 15 minutes until the juice from the tomatoes has been released. Season the tomatoes with salt and pepper and strain using a strainer with small holes in it to let some of the pulp drop through. Take 1 spoonful of the pesto sauce and add it to the tomato sauce.

Meanwhile, mix the spinach and mushrooms together with 1 tablespoon of grated parmesan cheese.

Place the wonton skins on a table. Place the filling in the middle and egg wash the sides.
Fold the skin in half so that you have a triangle. Take the two points and mound them together with a little egg wash.

Bring a pan of water to a boil. Place the tortellini-shaped wontons into the water, adding a little salt. Cook for 4 minutes until tender. Remove and place into a warmed serving bowl. Place the tomato pesto sauce on top and add some more grated parmesan cheese to the top of the dish. Serve and enjoy.

Spinach Gnocchi with Tomato and Tarragon Sauce

This is a great vegetarian entrée that the whole table can eat instead of meat.

Makes 6 servings

Ingredients

Gnocchi
4 large Idaho potatoes washed
3 oz butter
2 whole eggs
2 egg yolks
½ teaspoon of ground nutmeg
5oz all purpose flour
2 tablespoons of grated parmesan cheese

Sauce
¼ lb bag of fresh spinach
2 cloves of garlic, crushed and peeled
Salt and pepper to taste
2 tablespoons of shaved parmesan cheese (to garnish)
1 small bunch of chopped tarragon
6 large tomatoes, chopped

Method

Preheat oven to 350° F.
Place the potatoes on a baking sheet and bake for 1 hour until soft and tender.

Meanwhile, use a 2-quart saucepan to cook the onion and garlic until translucent. Add the chopped tomatoes and the tarragon. Cook for about 20 minutes, then strain through a large-hole strainer. Season with salt and pepper.

Remove the potatoes from the oven, cool, and cut the potatoes in half. Scoop out the potato from the skins. Mash the potatoes until very smooth, using a potato ricer or a simple masher. (You could make potato skins for a different dish.)

In a small mixing bowl, add the potatoes, nutmeg, flour, whole eggs, egg yolk, salt, and pepper. Mix well until smooth dough is made. Roll out onto a table and make small breadstick shapes, then cut into small pillow-looking shapes.

Heat a small pot of water to a boil. Place the gnocchi into the water and cook until they float, around 2-3 minutes. Remove from the heat, strain, and sauté in a little butter until golden brown. Add the spinach to the gnocchi, and stir in the tomato and tarragon sauce. Check for seasoning. Add a little more salt and pepper if desired.
Warm a large bowl. Place the gnocchi into the bowl and garnish with a little shaved parmesan. Serve and enjoy.

Don't be bashful about choosing your wine to go with the menu's that are in this book. Take the menu that you want to make and go to the supermarket or the wine store and ask them to match up the wine that goes with the food. So many people are not sure what goes with what and then try to match there own wine with it, but then it does not work for you!

We are in the business help, so ask us!

CHAPTER 4

SOME GUESTS COMING FOR A LIGHT SPRING DINNER

AND YOU WANT TO IMPRESS!!!!

Jumbo Lump Crab Cake with Vanilla Mango Chutney And Lemon Thyme Vinaigrette

I have had so many reviews of this crab cake, from people telling me it is better than any Maryland crab cake to the best crab cake in the world, enjoy it then you can have your discussions about it at the dinner table.

Makes 4 servings

Ingredients

Crab cake
1 lb can of jumbo lump crab meat
Zest and juice of ½ of a lemon
1 tablespoon of mayonnaise
½ cup of bread crumbs
1 tablespoon of blended oil
Salt and pepper

Mango chutney
2 mangoes, diced very small
1 vanilla bean (extract the seeds)
2 shallots, diced very small
1 tablespoon of chopped chives
1 tablespoon of white wine vinegar

Lemon vinaigrette
½ cup of white wine vinegar
Juice of 2 lemons
1 teaspoon of chopped thyme

Method

Crab Cake
Mix the crabmeat with the lemon zest, juice, mayonnaise, salt, pepper and bread crumbs. Do not over mix the crabmeat, otherwise it will break up. Mold into round cake shapes and dust with a little breadcrumb.

Preheat a non stick pan with a little blended oil, Sear the crab cakes until golden brown on each side, 2 minutes each side. Place in to preheated oven at 350f for 4 minutes until hot in the middle.

Serve over the mango chutney, and sprinkle with the lemon thyme vinaigrette.

Mango Chutney
In a mixing bowl, mix the mango with the vanilla bean, shallot, chive, and vinegar.

Lemon vinaigrette
In a bowl, mix the lemon juice with chopped thyme and slowly add the oil to emulsify.

Wild Oregon Salmon with Tarragon and Orange Risotto

Wild salmon is so much better in flavor then regular farm raised salmon, not only does it have a better color than farm raised it has a better taste as well, use Alaska wild salmon if you can get it, if not Oregon wild salmon is great.

Serves 4

Ingredients

4 6-oz. portions wild salmon
2 cups risotto rice (available at good supermarkets)
1½ small onion, diced, separated into two equal parts
4 cloves garlic, peeled and crushed
2 cups orange juice
1/4 cup orange juice
1/4 cup cream
4 cups water
2 oz. butter, cold
1 oz. fresh parmesan cheese, grated
1 oz. blended oil
Salt and pepper to taste
1 oz. white wine
1 stick of fresh tarragon
1 oz. of soft butter

Method

Preheat oven to 350° F.

Cook half the onion in the oil (keeping the rest of the onion for later) in a large pot. Add the garlic. Cook until translucent.

Coat the risotto in the sautéed onion and garlic mixture. Continue cooking.

When the rice becomes sticky, add water and 2 cups of orange juice to cover. Reduce heat until a slow simmer is achieved. Cook until rice is al dente, with a little bite to it. It is very important to stir constantly while the rice is cooking.

Season the rice with salt and pepper.

Cook the remaining onion with the white wine in a small saucepan.

Reduce heat. Add cream and butter very slowly to the wine reduction. Cook on a very low heat. Continue stirring for a smooth consistency.

When butter is completely incorporated, remove from the heat, season with salt and pepper. Remove from heat.

Season the salmon with salt and pepper. Pan-sear until golden brown.

Place into a preheated oven for about 5 minutes.

Put a little risotto — 2 spoons — into a small saucepan. Add 1/4 cup orange juice, tarragon, and 1 oz. of butter to make the risotto creamy, and then add in the parmesan cheese. Cook over low heat. Stir until thick and creamy.

To serve, place the risotto mixture on the middle of a plate. Place the salmon on top of the risotto. Spoon the sauce around the plate. Use a little tarragon stick for garnish.

Vanilla Crème Brulee

This is a great dessert every body loves crème brulee it is the simplest flavor but we all order this when we go out so try making this at home. Remember it takes about 6 hours to chill and set up.

Makes 6

Ingredients

2 cups of heavy whipping cream
5 egg yolks
3.75 oz of caster (superfine) sugar
2 fresh vanilla beans
2 oz. of brown cane sugar

Method

Bring the cream to a boil along with the vanilla bean (cut in half and scraped removing the seeds). In a mixing bowl, mix the egg yolks with the sugar until it turns white and creamy. Slowly add half of the boiling cream to the sugar mix. Mix in very well then add the remaining cream to the egg mix. Pour back into the saucepan, return to the heat, and keep stirring continuously on very low heat.

Once a little thickness has been achieved, pour into ramekins. Leave about 1 inch from the top.

Place the ramekins into a baking tray; add a little water to the baking tray and bake at 250° F for 55 minutes.

Check by touching the ramekin; if it seems a little runny still; continue cooking for about another 10 minutes and keep checking them.

Remove from the heat, cool down and store in refrigerator.
You must let the crème brulee set for about 4 hours to cool and set up.

To serve dust the brown sugar over the top. Burn using a kitchen torch until an even golden brown crust has been made. Serve and enjoy.

Asparagus Strudel, Frisee Salad, and Red Pepper Coulis

This is a great dish to impress your friends with, jumbo asparagus is better to use if you can find this, full of flavor and very easy to make.

Makes 4 servings

Ingredients

1 head of frisee lettuce (picked and washed)
3 bunches of asparagus (jumbo is better or thin)
1 whole egg
1 oz. of sesame seeds
2 sheets of puff pastry
1 cup of roasted red peppers
2 cloves of garlic, chopped
2 cups of blended oil
Salt and pepper to taste

Method

Cut the asparagus sticks in half. (Normally, if you pick up one piece of asparagus and snap it, it will tell you were to cut the asparagus.) Keep the bottoms for a soup.
Blanch the asparagus in boiling salted water. Remove and shock in ice water.
Roll out the puff pastry. Cut into 2-inch-by-2-inch squares; place the tops all in one direction. Brush the edges with egg wash, and then roll the bottom to make a parcel.
Brush the top with egg wash and dust with the sesame seeds just for presentation.
Place onto a greased baking sheet and put into a preheated oven at 350 degrees for 10 minutes.

Using a food processor, add the chopped garlic puree for 10 seconds, and then add the roasted red pepper to the garlic. Continue to make a smooth paste. Slowly add the blended oil to the food processor. Remove and check the seasoning; add more if needed.

In a small bowl, add the lettuce, season with salt and pepper, and a small drizzle of oil.
Place the lettuce in the middle of a chilled plate. Then place the asparagus strudel on top of the lettuce. Spoon the red pepper coulis around the plate. Serve and enjoy.

Spring Lamb Chops with Celery Root Potato and Mint Sauce

This may seem like a complicated dish to make, but the reward of the great lamb taste and mint sauce is just great. If you can find the whole racks of lamb, this is the best way to go. Just grill them whole then place them in the oven until your desired temperature is achieved. Slice them after they are cooked.

Serves 4

Ingredients

2 large lamb racks, or 12 chops (available at most supermarkets or good butchers)
4 large Yukon gold potatoes
½ large onion, peeled
3 cups of cream
1 cup of red wine
2 small shallots, diced fine
½ cup of butter
Salt and pepper
¼ cup of blended oil
1 cube of beef stock dissolved to make 2 cups of stock
1 bunch of fresh mint, chopped in to thin strips
1 bunch of fresh broccoli, boiled and kept warm
1 bulb celery root (Most supermarkets have these in stock.)

Method

Peel the celery root, dice finely, and boil with a little salt and water (enough to cover).

Once cooked, strain, and if you have a food processor, blend the celery root with a little butter and cream. If you do not have a food processor, use a regular masher. You may want to overcook the celery root. Reserve when finished.

Peel and dice the potatoes. In a large pot, cook the potatoes in water and a little salt.

Once cooked, strain and dry the potatoes by returning them to the heat. Mash the potatoes and add a little of the cream and half of the butter stated above until your desired consistency of mashed potatoes has been achieved. Add the celery root puree from above. Remember to season the potatoes with salt and pepper.

Preheat a grill or a nonstick pan with a little oil and then place the seasoned (salt and pepper) lamb chops on the grill/pan for 5 minutes, turning occasionally. Then place in preheated oven at 450f for 10 minutes or until desired doneness. Remember to rest all meat before you eat it; it will taste better. (To rest means, that you must remove from the heat and let the meat relax, it will taste better and the meat will not be tough unless it is overcooked)

Take 1 cup of red wine and the shallots, and reduce in a small pan. Once reduced, add the beef stock and the chopped mint.

When the sauce has reduced, add a little nugget of butter, about a half ounce, to bring the sauce all together.

On a warmed plate, place the mashed potato in the middle, then place the lamb chops on top and spoon the sauce around the plate. Place the broccoli on top. Enjoy.

Warm Peach Tart Tatin with Vanilla Ice Cream

This is a great spring dessert dish. Peaches are great seasonal fruit, Georgia and South Carolina have some of the best peaches I have tried, this recipe seems complicated but is very easy and your guests will be impressed.

Makes 4

Ingredients

2 ripe whole peaches
1 sheet of puff pastry
3 oz. of brown sugar
3 oz. of soft butter
1 egg, beaten, for egg wash
1 pint of fresh vanilla ice cream from a grocery store

Method

Preheat oven to 350 degrees.

Cut the peaches in half and remove the stone. Fan the peach halves, so as to make shape of the Chinese hand held fan.

Using a pie tin dish, add the butter and brown sugar. Place onto a low heat until a golden brown caramel is made. Then place the peach half in a fancy pattern of your choice.

Roll out the puff pastry until large enough to cover the pie tin. Place over the peaches, brush with egg wash, and place into the oven for 25 minutes.

Remove from the oven very carefully; place to cool down for about 5 minutes.
Turn upside down and place onto a plate.

You can serve this dessert family style, so that everyone can help themselves to this, or you can serve this individually. Serve the ice cream right on top of the peach tart and enjoy.

Some great sunsets in Colorado, with all the mountains in the back ground

CHAPTER 5

SOME GUESTS COMING FOR A SUMMER NIGHT

AND YOU WANT TO IMPRESS!!!!

Dungeness Crab and Apple Tower with Lemon Thyme Vinaigrette

Dungeness crab is a sweeter crab very small, this crab goes so well with fruit flavors it is a great dish with the apple, and lemon vinaigrette, enjoy

Makes 4 servings

Ingredients

1 lb. of Dungeness crab meat (picked clean of shells)
Juice of ½ a lemon
1 tablespoon of mayonnaise
2 granny smith apples
1 tsp. of chopped fresh chives
Salt and pepper

Lemon vinaigrette
½ cup of white wine vinegar
Juice of 2 lemons
1 teaspoon of chopped thyme

Method

Crab Tower

Mix the crabmeat with the lemon Juice, mayonnaise, chives, salt, and pepper in a small bowl. Peel the apples and core the middle using a corer. Slice very thin, about 1 mm thick; sprinkle a little lemon juice to prevent them from going brown.

Use a cookie cutter (large round cutter about 3 inches wide and 2 inches high). Place a spoonful of the crab mix into the cutter, then place an apple slice on top of that. Repeat until you have about three layers.

To serve, place onto a chilled plate. Remove the cookie cutter. You can use a little lettuce sprinkled around the plate as in the picture. Sprinkle the lemon vinaigrette around the plate.

Lemon vinaigrette
In a bowl, mix the lemon juice with chopped thyme and slowly add the oil to emulsify.

Pan-roasted Free Range Chicken, Spinach Potato And Tarragon Sauce

This is nice summer entrée. This can be a show-off dish that is really simple. Free range chicken is so much better to use; better flavor.

Serves 4

Ingredients

4 6-oz. free range chicken breasts (available at most supermarkets or good butchers on pre-order)
4 large Yukon gold potatoes
2 large onions, peeled
2 cup of cream
2 cups of fresh spinach
1 tablespoon of prepared coarse-grain mustard
1 cup of red wine
2 cubes of chicken stock (or 1 cup of fresh chicken stock)
¼ cup of butter
Salt and pepper
¼ cup of oil

Method

Peel and dice the potatoes. In a large pot, cook the potatoes in water and a little salt. Once cooked, strain and dry the potatoes by returning them to the heat. Mash the potatoes and add a little of the cream and half of the butter stated above until your desired consistency of mashed potatoes has been achieved.

In a small pot, boil 2 cups of water. Add the spinach to that. Once cooked, remove and place into ice water. Strain and place into a food processor and make a puree. Add the spinach puree to the potatoes; remember to season the potatoes with salt and pepper.

Pre-warm a grill or a nonstick pan with a little blended oil, and then place the seasoned (salt and pepper) chicken breast on the grill/pan for 5 minutes, turning occasionally. Then place in preheated oven at 350f for 10 minutes.

Take 1 cup of red wine and reduce in a small pan. Add the chicken stock to that. Reduce and add the tarragon to the sauce and butter. When the sauce has thickened, remove from heat.

On a warmed plate, place the mashed potato in the middle, then place the chicken breast on top and spoon the sauce around the plate. Enjoy

Rhubarb Crumble with Vanilla Ice Cream

This is a great dish for a summer evening; rhubarb is a late spring summer fruit, looks like celery but it is red and longer than celery, great flavor. The crumble is very similar to a streusel topping.

Makes 6

Ingredients

For the topping

8oz all purpose flour
10oz soft butter
10oz caster sugar

Rhubarb stew

2 lb. of fresh rhubarb
1 pint of fresh blackberries
2 oz butter
2 oz brown sugar
1 tsp. of ground cinnamon
1 tsp. of vanilla extract
1 pint of vanilla ice cream (store bought)

Method

Preheat a nonstick pan. Also preheat oven to 350° F.

Peel the rhubarb to remove the outer skin. Chop the rhubarb into small pieces.

Add the butter to the nonstick pan, and then add the cinnamon, vanilla extract, brown sugar, and the rhubarb. Continue to cook the rhubarb until soft and tender. Remove and place into a glass Pyrex dish.

In a small mixing bowl, mix the butter, flour, and sugar together, until it resembles cake crumbs. Sprinkle the crumbs over the rhubarb mix and place in the oven for 25 minutes.

Remove from the oven when a golden crust has been achieved. Serve on a small round plate with a scoop of vanilla ice cream. Enjoy the great flavors.

Goat Cheese and Chive Spring Roll with Pesto Dressing

This is a great dish to impress your friends. You need deep fryer for this dish. You can make your own deep fryer using a deep pan and a thermometer.

Makes 4 servings

Ingredients

1 packet of egg roll wrappers (available at grocery stores)
1 6oz log of goat cheese
1 bunch of fresh chives
1 whole egg
2 cups of baby spinach
4 cups of blended oil

Pesto dressing
2 cups of fresh basil
1 clove of fresh garlic, peeled
¼ cup of fresh grated parmesan cheese
1 cup of blended oil
¼ cup of toasted pine nuts
Salt and pepper to taste

Combine all ingredients and blend in a food processor to make a smooth paste.

Method

In a food processor, add the goat cheese and blend into a smooth paste. Finely chop the chives and these to the goat cheese paste in the food processor. Remove from the food processor.

Place the egg roll wrappers on the table. Spoon the goat cheese in a line on the egg roll wrapper. Brush the sides with egg wash, fold them over, then brush the ends with the egg wash, and roll up into a big cigar shape.

Preheat the deep fryer to 350 degrees using your thermometer. Place the spring roll into the deep fryer, keeping an eye on it. Remove when it becomes crispy, normally about 2 minutes.

Let the spring roll cool for a short while before cutting it. Place the baby spinach in the middle of a plate then cut the spring roll in half. Spoon the pesto dressing around the plate. Serve and enjoy.

Poached Halibut with Red Pepper Couscous and Spinach Sauce

This is a great dish. Fresh halibut comes into season around the end of March through October. Poaching just increases the great flavor it has already. Israeli couscous is big grains of pasta, like the regular, smaller couscous, which is from Morocco.

Serves 4

Ingredients

4 6-oz. portions of halibut filet
2 cups of Israeli couscous
1½ small onions, diced fine
4 cloves of peeled garlic, crushed
1 small can of roasted red pepper, peeled and pureed to make a smooth paste
¼ cup of cream
8 cups of water
2 oz. of butter, cold
1 oz. of grated fresh parmesan cheese
1 oz. of blended oil
Salt and pepper
3 cups of white wine
2 oz. of fresh spinach

Method

In a large pot, cook half the onion in the oil. Add the garlic and cook until translucent. Add the couscous and cook until coated in the onion and garlic. When the couscous becomes sticky, add 6 cups of water and turn the heat down until a slow simmer is achieved. Season the couscous with salt and pepper. It is very important that you keep stirring the couscous. When it is cooked, it should be al dente with a little bite to it.
Normal cooking time is about 15 minutes.

In small pan, cook the 1 cup of white wine with the spinach. Add the cream to the wine reduction. Using a drink blender, add all the sauce to it and blend. Strain and season the sauce with salt and pepper. Reserve for later with no heat.

Season the halibut with salt and pepper, then place the halibut into the poaching liquid.
Using a flat Pyrex glass dish with 2 cups of water and 2 cups of white wine, cover the halibut with foil and cook for 8 minutes.

Take a little couscous in a small pan. Add a little more water, red pepper puree, and butter until thick and creamy.

To serve, place the couscous in the middle of the plate, then place the halibut on top of the couscous. Spoon the sauce around the plate and serve and enjoy.

Strawberry Crepe with Crème Chantilly

What a summer fruit strawberries are, using them in a crepe seals in the entire flavor in sweet dough, and a vanilla cream wow! enjoy.

Makes 6.

Ingredients

½ cup heavy whipping cream
2 tablespoons of vanilla extract
2 oz. of sugar
1 pint of fresh strawberries
4oz of all purpose flour
1 egg
½ pint of fresh milk

Method

In a small mixing bowl, mix the flour with the egg; add the milk and 1 oz. of sugar. Mix in very well until a smooth batter is made. Preheat a nonstick frying pan. Place a little oil in the pan and add the batter to make a small, thin layer crepe. Turn over when small bubbles appear in the crepe. Remove the crepe from the heat and place in between sheets of greased paper.

In another small mixing bowl, wash the strawberries and cut them into quarters. Place the strawberries into the crepes and roll them up into thin cigar shapes. I would use two per serving, as these are nice and light.

Whisk up the cream until nice and thick. Add the sugar and vanilla extract.

To serve, place the crepes in the middle of a chilled plate. Spoon the vanilla crème over the strawberry crepe. Serve and enjoy.

What do all the flowers mean in the book, like the one on the opposite page?

They are supposed to represent the seasons and the new chapter.

I have chosen the colors to represent the four seasons.

Spring bright yellow
Summer a nice summer bluebell flower
Fall a nice orange and red flower to represent the leaves falling
And winter last but not least the white for the snow and the cold.

I hope you are enjoying the book so far.

CHAPTER 6

THE LEAVES ARE CHANGING COLOR.
COME GET WARM

AND YOU WANT TO IMPRESS!!!!

Forest Mushroom Soup with Truffle Cream

This is a great soup for a cold winter night or you just want to impress your friends with smells this one will get the house smelling good.

Makes 6 servings

Ingredients

2 shallots, peeled and finely sliced
1 stick of celery, washed and sliced thin
1 lb. of fresh shiitake mushrooms or crimini mushrooms
2 large potatoes, peeled and chopped into a dice
4 cloves of garlic, chopped or crushed
2 cups of vegetable stock (you can use cubes from supermarkets for this)
¼ cup of oil
2 tablespoons of truffle oil
4 cups of heavy whipping cream
Salt and pepper to taste

Method

In a large pot, cook the shallots, garlic, and potatoes in a small amount of oil.
Chop the mushrooms, using the bottoms and the tops. Just rinse if a little dirty, continue cooking for 10 minutes.

Add the vegetable stock over the ingredients in the pot and simmer for 35 minutes.
Puree using a stick blender or a drink blender, but be careful not to fill it too much.
Strain the soup using a fine strainer. Season the soup and check the consistency.
Add 2 cups of cream to the soup after it is strained.

In a small mixing bowl, add the remaining cream and whip until thick consistency.
Add the 2 tablespoons of truffle oil. This may seem very strong, but the potency will disappear after a while, and you want to impress your guests with the aroma.

Pour the soup into preheated serving bowls. Garnish with a little of the truffle cream drizzled around. Serve and enjoy.

Roast Veal Chop with Truffle Risotto

Veal has such a great flavor, mix this with truffle what a great combination. The foie gras sauce really sets this dish to being a great entertaining plate.

Serves 4

Ingredients

4 large 8-oz. veal chops (available at most supermarkets or good butchers on pre-order)
2 cups of risotto rice
1 small onion, diced fine
4 cloves of peeled garlic, crushed
1 oz. of truffle oil
2 oz. of foie gras pureed in a food processor with 1 oz. of butter
4 cups of chicken stock
2 oz. of butter, cold
1 oz. of grated fresh parmesan cheese
1 oz. of blended oil
Salt and pepper
4 oz. of veal stock (available at most supermarkets)
12 pieces of grilled asparagus

Method

In a large pot, sauté the onion in the oil. Add the garlic and cook until translucent. Add the risotto rice and cook until coated in the onion and garlic. When the rice becomes sticky, add the chicken stock to cover, and turn the heat down until a slow simmer is achieved. Season the rice with salt and pepper. It is very important that you keep stirring the rice. When it is cooked, it should be al dente with a little bite to it.

Pre-warm a nonstick sauté pan, and place the seasoned veal chops in and roast for 15 minutes, turning occasionally.

Warm the veal stock, add the foie gras butter to the stock and stir until it has a nice shiny appearance.

On a warmed plate, place the risotto in the middle, then place the veal chop on top and spoon the sauce around the plate. Place the grilled asparagus on top.

Orange Crème Brulee

This is another great dish that sells very well, very similar to the vanilla crème brulee, except it has the orange flavor. Remember this takes 5 hours to chill and set up.

Makes 6

Ingredients

2 cups of heavy whipping cream at
5 egg yolks
3.75 oz caster (superfine) sugar
2 fresh vanilla beans
1 orange, zested with a fine grater
1 oz. of orange liqueur (Grand Marnier) optional
2 oz. of brown cane sugar

Method

Bring the cream to a boil along with the orange zest, vanilla bean, (cut in half and scraped, removing the seeds).

In a mixing bowl, mix the egg yolks with the sugar until it turns white and creamy. (Add the orange liqueur if desired.)

Slowly add half of the boiling cream to the sugar mix. Mix in very well, and then add the remaining cream to the egg mix. Pour back into the saucepan, return to the heat, on very low heat, and keep stirring continuously.

Once a little thickness has been achieved, pour into ramekins. Leave about 1 inch from the top. Place the ramekins into a baking tray; add a little water to the baking tray.
Bake at 250° F for 55 minutes.

Check by touching the ramekin; if it seems a little runny still; continue cooking for about another 10 minutes. Keep checking them.

Remove from the heat, cool down, and store in a refrigerator. You must let the crème brulee set for about 4 hours to cool and set up.

To serve, dust the brown sugar over the top. Burn using a kitchen torch until an even golden brown crust has been made. Serve and enjoy.

Potato Crusted Foie Gras, Pear Chutney and a Cherry Sauce

This is a great dish for a very impressive dinner. I suggest that you make this dish for yourself beforehand, to make sure that you can make it well for your guests. Enjoy.

Serves 4

Ingredients

4 large 2-oz. pieces of foie gras
2 large Yukon gold potatoes, peeled
1 whole egg, beaten
1 tablespoon of corn starch
2 large Bosc pears (peeled and diced in lemon water)
1 small shallot, diced
¼ cup of oil
1 tsp. of ground cinnamon
1 cup of orange juice
1 cup of cherry liqueur
½ cup of fresh or dry cherries
Salt and pepper

Method

Using a Japanese mandolin and a potato shredder attachment, grate the potatoes. Place into a dish towel to remove the excess water. Season the potatoes.

Place the foie gras into the egg mix and coat very well. Then dust in the corn starch, and place into the potato mix. Wrap the potato around the foie gras until it has an even coating. Place the wrapped foie gras into the refrigerator until it becomes hard.

In a small saucepan, reduce the orange juice and cherry liqueur until thick syrup is achieved. Add the cherries to the mix and store to improve the flavor.

In a small bowl, mix the diced pear with the diced shallots and cinnamon. Place into a small sauté pan with a little oil, and cook until the pear is soft. Preheat a heavy sauté pan, place a little oil in the pan, then add the foie gras, turning when golden brown. Place into a preheated oven at 350f for 5 minutes until foie gras is soft.

To plate, place the pear chutney in the middle of the plate; place the seared foie gras on top of the pear and spoon a little of the sauce around the plate. Serve and enjoy.

Pecan-crusted Venison Loin, Apple Potato Puree and a Blackberry Sauce

This is a great dish for the real meat eaters who like game and venison; this can really impress people for a dinner party or just to make for a gathering of people.

Serves 4

Ingredients

4 6-oz. portions of venison loin (available at a good butcher)
4 granny smith apples (peeled and diced, and stored in lemon water)
4 large peeled potatoes (diced)
2 oz. of soft butter
2 oz. of cream
Salt and pepper to taste
1 tablespoon of Dijon mustard
2 oz. of toasted pecans (ground in a food processor)
1 bunch of baby beets, peeled and blanched
1 oz. of fresh blackberries
½ cup of venison sauce (recipe below)
1 oz. of blended oil

Method

Season the venison with salt and pepper, Then pan sear the venison loin in the oil. Once seared, remove from the heat and brush with the Dijon mustard and sprinkle the pecan crumbs over the venison.

Place onto a small baking tray and finish in the oven at 350f or until desired temperature you want. (Medium rare is my favorite, 5-6 minutes.)

Cook the potatoes in water and a little salt. When ¾ of the way cooked, add the chopped apples to the pot. When the apples and potatoes are cooked enough to mash, place them in a food processor with a little cream and butter. Keep warm.

Crisp the baby beets in a little butter until golden brown, and season with salt and pepper. Remove the venison from the oven and let it rest for 5 minutes. (It relaxes the meat so it will be tender.)

Serve on a warmed plate. Spoon the potato in the middle of the plate, and slice the venison into a couple of small medallions. Sprinkle the baby beets around the plate, place a few of the blackberries around the plate, and pour a spoonful of the sauce around and over the meat. Serve and enjoy.

Venison Sauce
Ingredients

1cup of venison trimmings
1 large carrot, peeled
1 stalk of washed celery
2 cloves of garlic, peeled and crushed
1 cup of red wine, cabernet my preference
1 sprig of thyme
1 oz. of blackberries
Salt and pepper
1 oz. of blended oil
2 cups of chicken stock (you can make with cubes if you'd like)

Method

In a thick-bottom pan, cook the venison trimmings in a little oil until golden brown.
Cut the carrots and celery into a small dice. Add these to the venison trimmings in the pan.
Add the thyme and garlic, and cook until brown. Deglaze the pan with the red wine.
Reduce until a small covering of wine is left. Cover with a little chicken stock and reduce; add the blackberries to add flavor.
When the back of a spoon is coated well, strain through a fine strainer and store until ready to present the dish.

Banana Bread Pudding with Vanilla Custard

This is a great dish for fall, which can really impress people for a dinner party or just to make for a gathering of people.

Makes 6

Ingredients

1 loaf of white bread (remove the crusts)
2 pints of skim milk
1 teaspoon of vanilla extract
6 whole eggs
7 oz of caster (superfine) sugar
3 bananas

Method

Bring the milk and vanilla to a boil and stir very well. Remove from the heat.
In a mixing bowl, mix the whole egg and sugar together, then add the hot milk over the sugar. Mix very well.

Using a flat glass Pyrex dish spread it with a little butter to prevent sticking. Lay the bread one slice per layer, and then add the chopped bananas over that. Repeat this until you have made three layers. Pour the milk/egg liquid over the bread pudding.

Place foil over the pudding and place in a preheated oven at 250 degrees for 35 minutes.
Check by using a small fork. If there is still a little custard on the fork, return for another 10 minutes. Remove the foil and place back into the oven to brown for 5 minutes. Remove from the heat. Cut a 2-inch square, and lift it out using a fish slice. Serve with a spoonful of vanilla custard.

Vanilla custard
Ingredients
2 cups of milk
6oz caster (superfine) sugar
5 egg yolks
1 fresh vanilla bean

Method

Boil the milk and vanilla bean.

In a small mixing bowl, beat the egg yolks with the sugar until white and creamy. Slowly add the boiling milk over the egg, and return to the heat, (very low, otherwise you will separate the custard). Use the back of a wooden spoon to keep stirring very often. Once it has thickened, it will coat the back of the spoon. Strain, pour into a container, and then place the strained custard into an ice bath to cool down very fast.

Cold winter days in Colorado, and all that snow.

CHAPTER 7

YOU HAVE GUESTS ARRIVING A NEED TO BE WARMED UP.

AND YOU WANT TO IMPRESS!!!!

Curried Butternut Squash Soup with Chive Crème Friache

This is a great soup for a cold winter's night or if you just want to impress your friends with smells. This one will get the house smelling good, and with the spices it will warm you up.

Makes 6 servings

Ingredients

2 shallots, peeled and finely sliced
1 stalk of celery, washed and sliced thin
2 lb. of butternut squash
2 large potatoes, peeled and chopped into a dice
4 cloves of garlic, chopped or crushed
2 cups of vegetable stock (you can use cubes from the supermarket for this)
¼ cup of oil
2 tablespoons of madras curry powder
1 cup of crème fraiche
1 oz. of fresh chopped chives
Salt and pepper to taste

Method

Use a large pot. Cook the shallots, garlic, potatoes, in a small amount of oil. Peel and chop the butternut squash, and add to the shallot and potato mix, along with the curry powder. Continue cooking for 10 minutes.

Add the vegetable stock over the ingredients in the pot simmer for 35 minutes. Puree using a stick blender or a drink blender, but be careful not to fill it too much. Strain the soup, using a fine strainer. Season the soup and check the consistency.

In a small mixing bowl, add the crème fraiche, chives, salt and pepper. Mix well until smooth cream is made.

Pour the soup into preheated serving bowls. Garnish with a little of the chive crème friache drizzled around. Serve and enjoy.

Roast Beef Wellington with Horseradish Potato And Red Wine Sauce

This is one of my favorites; the guests' eyes will light up when you bring this to the table. This may be an expensive dish to make, but worth every penny. This is my version of the great British dish beef Wellington.

Serves 4

Ingredients

1 beef tenderloin, whole, cleaned (Ask your butcher to do this.)
4 large Yukon gold potatoes
2 tablespoons of prepared horseradish
½ large onion, peeled
1 cup of red wine
2 small shallots, diced fine
½ cup of butter
Salt and pepper
¼ cup of oil
1 cube of beef stock, dissolved to make 2 cups of stock
1 bunch of fresh broccoli, boiled and kept warm
1 sheet of puff pastry
1 tablespoon of Dijon mustard
1 whole egg, beaten

Method

Peel and dice the potatoes. In a large pot, cook the potatoes in water and a little salt.
Once cooked, strain and dry the potatoes by returning them to the heat. Mash the potatoes and add a little of the cream and half of the butter stated above until your desired consistency of mashed potatoes has been achieved. Add the horseradish. Remember to season the potatoes with salt and pepper.

Pre-warm a grill or a nonstick pan with a little oil and then place the seasoned (salt and pepper) whole beef tenderloin on the grill/pan for 5 minutes, turning occasionally. Then remove from the heat and let the beef cool down. Remember to rest all meat before you eat it; it will taste better.

Brush the beef tenderloin with the Dijon mustard. Roll in the puff pastry and brush the edge with the egg wash. Seal and place into a preheated oven at 350° F for15 minutes, or until desired temperature is achieved.

Take 1 cup of red wine, and the shallots, and reduce in a small pan. Once reduced, add the beef stock. When the sauce has reduced, add a little nugget of butter, about half an ounce, to bring the sauce all together.

On a warmed plate, place the mashed potato in the middle, then slice the beef and place it on top of the potatoes. Place the broccoli on top. Enjoy.

Flourless Chocolate Fondant Cake

This is a great dish that can really impress people for a dinner party or just to make for a gathering of people. Remember that this dish takes 4 hours to set the ganache.

Makes 6 servings

Chocolate Ganache
Ingredients

1½ lb. of dark chocolate
2 cups of heavy whipping cream
Zest of 1 orange

Bring the cream and the other ingredients to a boil and stir very well. Remove from the heat and store in the refrigerator for about 4 hours until the mix becomes very hard.

Cake Filling
Ingredients

7 oz. of dark chocolate
7 oz. of butter
6 oz. of egg yolk
4 whole eggs
5 oz. of powdered sugar
1 pint of Vanilla ice cream (store bought)

Method

Mix the butter and chocolate together in a small mixing bowl, place the bowl over a small pan of boiling water, until the chocolate starts to melt with the butter, remove from the heat.
In a mixing bowl, mix the egg yolks with the whole eggs and the 5 oz. of sugar until it turns white and creamy. Slowly mix in the chocolate mix to the sugar mix.

When this is done, check the chocolate ganache that you made earlier. It must be thick or hard by the time you want to use this. If it is set, scoop out using a teaspoon, making around 1-cm balls of chocolate.

Scoop the chocolate batter into a buttered and floured foil container, ramekin shape.
Place the chocolate ball into the middle of the batter and bake at 450° F for 10 minutes.
Remove from the heat; let the cake stand for 2 minutes. Turn upside down and scoop a ball of vanilla ice cream. Serve and enjoy.

Pan Seared Diver Scallops with Saffron Risotto

I would ask the fishmonger or a good grocery store for the large diver caught scallops, they are a little more expensive but well worth the flavor

Serves 4

Ingredients

8 large bay diver caught scallops (available from a good seafood supplier or supermarket on a pre-order)
2 cups of risotto rice
1½ small onions, diced fine
4 cloves of peeled garlic, crushed
1 pinch of saffron
Juice of 1 lemon
¼ cup of cream
4 cups of water
2 oz. of butter, cold
1 oz. of grated fresh parmesan cheese
1 oz. of blended oil
Salt and pepper
1 oz. of white wine

Method

In a large pot, sauté one onion in the oil, keeping the remainder of the onion for later. Add the garlic and cook until translucent. Add the risotto rice and cook until coated in the onion and garlic. Add the pinch of saffron. When the rice becomes sticky, add the water to cover. Turn the heat down until a slow simmer is achieved. Season the rice with salt and pepper.
It is very important that you keep stirring the rice. When it is cooked, it should be al dente with a little bite to it.

In another small pan, cook the remaining onion with the white wine. Squeeze the lemon juice into the reduction. Add the cream to the sauce and the butter. Keep stirring so that the butter does not break.(You do not want the heat to hot it will make the butter and cream separate, this causes this to break, not good because it will become to runny)
Season the sauce with salt and pepper.
Season the scallops with salt and pepper, then pan sear the scallops until golden brown.
Take a little risotto in a small pan add a little more stock and butter and then add in the parmesan cheese until thick and creamy.

To plate, place the risotto in the middle of the plate and then place the scallops around the plate. Spoon the sauce around the plate and serve.

Marinated Duck Breast with Napa Cabbage and Raspberry Sauce

Duck has such a great flavor you could buy the whole duck and then use the legs for a different use. This is a nice and fruity winter dish; looks like a lot, but is not overly filling.

Serves 4

Ingredients

4 large 6-oz. duck breasts (available at most supermarkets or good butchers on pre-order)
1 head of Napa cabbage (Napa cabbage is a large green cabbage very good for stir fry's)
2 small onions, diced fine
1 clove of peeled garlic, crushed
1 oz. of bacon, cut into thin strips
2 oz. of butter, cold
1 oz. of fresh raspberries
1 oz. of blended oil
1 cup of good balsamic vinegar
2 oz. dry figs
Salt and pepper
4 oz. of veal stock (available at most supermarkets)

Method

Cut the cabbage into thin strips.
In a large pot, cook the onion in one ounce of oil and add the garlic. Cook until translucent. Add the cabbage and cook until tender; you may want to add a small half cup of water, and this will reduced the size of the cabbage by half.

Marinate the duck breast. Take a plastic quart bag; place the duck in the bag for about 20 minutes with the balsamic vinegar, ½ oz. of blended oil, and the dry figs. Season the duck with salt and pepper. It is very important that you keep shaking the bag of duck so that it gets an even marinade.
In a small saucepan, cook the remaining onion, deglaze with the red wine, and reduce by ¾. Add the veal stock and reduce again by half, then add the raspberries, strain and serve later with the duck.
Pre-warm a nonstick sauté pan, then place the seasoned duck breast into the pan and roast for 5 minutes, turning each side.

Place into preheated oven at 450f for 8 minutes or until your desired liking. (Medium rare is my choice.) Add the figs to the pan now. If you add too early, they will get too caramelized.
On a warmed plate, place the cabbage in the middle, then place the duck breast on top and spoon the sauce around the plate. Place the figs around the plate. Serve and enjoy.

Port Poached Pear with Cinnamon Whipped Cream

Pears are a great winter fruit if they seem a little hard when you buy them for this dish that is fine because you are going to poach them with the port.
This is a really good dish for the winter a little like mulled wine instead made with port.

Makes 4

Ingredients

2 large Bosc pears (Bosc pears have a better flavor)
3 cups of cooking port
1 cinnamon stick
2 oz caster sugar (superfine) sugar
2 cups of heavy whipping cream
1 orange, zested with a fine grater
1 teaspoon of ground cinnamon

Method

Peel the pears and remove the seeds out of the middle using a corer. Place into a small saucepan. Cover with the port, cinnamon stick, and the orange zest. Place a lid on the pears so that the steam helps to poach the pears.

Continue to cook for 25 minutes until the pears are tender. Remove the pears from the pan and reduce the poaching liquor until it becomes thick syrup. Strain and set aside.

In a small mixing bowl, add the whipping cream, sugar, and ground cinnamon. Whip until thick.

To serve, cut the pears in half so you have four portions. Slice the bottom parts so it looks like a fan. Place onto a chilled plate. Sprinkle the reduced syrup around the plate, then spoon the cinnamon whipped cream on top and garnish with powdered sugar and a mint sprig. Serve and enjoy.

ABOUT THE AUTHOR

Steve has such a passion about food you can see this when you look at the pictures in his book.

He has so many people asking about if he has a cook book available, when they eat in his restaurant.

Well here it is his debut book, **So You Want to Impress!!!!**

Steve cares so much about food that is all he thinks about all day long, when he goes home he does not want to eat any food, he just looks at books thinks about what he can do next with food.

Steve lives for people to enjoy his food, when he sees people enjoying with big smiles it makes it all worth while.

It could be that dinner party that he is doing, or if it is the restaurant that he working in, he is trying to impress people all the time.

Steve is originally from Portsmouth, England.

He loves to rub in the fact that people always say "you're from England and they do not know how to cook food so what happened to you" all you have to do is look at his food and you know different.

Steve has been to many places in the world to see different types of food, Spain, France, Austria, Canada and not last USA.

All the different regions of the United States, makes a interesting life for any cook, but Steve sees so many different types of food, from all these areas Northwest, Northeast, Deep South, Southwest, Southeast and the middle of the country, he has to try that region of food.

Now residing in the United States, Vail, Colorado the beautiful Rocky Mountains,

Enjoy this book with him and try the recipes, have a go.